COLLECTORS
EDITION

ISBN 1440470960

michelle obama

In Her Own Words

THE SPEECHES 2008

Compiled by Susan A. Jones

Introduction: About Michelle

Michelle LaVaughn Obama, née Robinson, (born January 17, 1964) is an American attorney and the wife of Barack Obama, current President-elect of the United States and former Senator from Illinois. She will be the first African-American to become the First Lady of the United States.

She was born and grew up on the South Side of Chicago and graduated from Princeton University and Harvard Law School. After completing her formal education, she returned to Chicago and accepted a position with the law firm Sidley Austin, and subsequently worked as part of the staff of Chicago mayor Richard M. Daley, and for the University of Chicago Medical Center.

Michelle Obama is the sister of Craig Robinson, men's basketball coach at Oregon State University. She met Barack Obama when he joined Sidley Austin. After his election to the U.S. Senate, the Obama family continued to live on Chicago's South Side, choosing to remain there rather than moving to Washington, D.C..

Michelle Robinson was born on January 17, 1964, in Chicago, Illinois to Fraser Robinson III (who died in 1991), a city water plant employee and Democratic precinct captain, and Marian Shields Robinson, a secretary at Spiegel's catalog store. Michelle can trace her roots to pre-Civil War African Americans in the American South; her paternal great-great grandfather, Jim Robinson, was an American slave in the state of South Carolina, where some of her family still reside. She grew up in the South Shore community area of Chicago, and was raised in a conventional two-parent home. The family ate meals together and also entertained together as a family by playing games such as Monopoly and by reading. She and her brother, Craig (who is 21 months older), skipped the second grade. By sixth grade, Michelle joined a gifted class at Bryn Mawr Elementary School (later renamed Bouchet Academy). She attended Whitney Young High School, Chicago's first magnet high school, where she was on the honor roll four years, took advanced placement classes, was a member of the National Honor Society and served as student council treasurer. She was a high school classmate of Santita Jackson, the daughter of Jesse Jackson and sister of Jesse Jackson, Jr. She graduated from high school in 1981, and went on to major in sociology and minor in African American studies at Princeton University, where she graduated cum laude with a Bachelor of Arts in 1985.

At Princeton, she challenged the teaching methodology for French because she felt that it should be more conversational. As part of her requirements for graduation, she wrote a thesis entitled, "Princeton-Educated Blacks and the Black Community." She obtained her Juris Doctor (J.D.) degree from Harvard Law School in 1988. While at Harvard, she participated in political demonstrations advocating the hiring of professors who are members of minorities.

Barack and Michelle Obama

She met Barack Obama when they were among very few African Americans at their law firm (she has sometimes said only two, although others have pointed out there were others in different departments) and she was assigned to mentor him while he was a summer associate. Their relationship started with a business lunch and then a community organization meeting where he first impressed her. The couple's first date was to the Spike Lee movie Do the Right Thing. The couple married in October 1992, and they have two daughters, Malia Ann (born 1998) and Natasha (known as Sasha) (born 2001). Throughout her husband's 2008 campaign for President of the United States, she has made a "commitment to be away overnight only once a week — to campaign only two days a week and be home by the end of the second day" for their two children. The marital relationship has had its ebbs and flows according to public account. Barack recalled that their first kiss tasted like chocolate. However, the combination of an evolving family life and beginning political career led to many arguments about balancing work and family. In fact, he wrote in his second book, The Audacity of Hope: Thoughts on Reclaiming the American Dream, that "Tired and stressed, we had little time for conversation, much less romance". Now, in addition to the conflict of work and family, Michelle has to deal with the celebrity issues of "being married to a man some adore as a political superstar." according to an appearance on the October 3, 2006 Oprah Winfrey Show.

She once requested that Barack, who was then her fiancé, meet her prospective boss, Valerie Jarrett, when considering her first career move. Now, Jarrett is one of her husband's closest advisors. Early in the presidential race, Michelle Obama did not portray herself as an advisor to her husband. In fact, she was quoted in interviews saying "My job is not a senior advisor."

The Obamas` daughters attend the University of Chicago Lab School, which is a private school. According to an Obama interview on the 2008 season premiere of The Ellen DeGeneres Show, the couple does not intend to have any more children.

Career

Following law school, she was an associate at the Chicago office of the law firm Sidley Austin, where she first met her husband. At the firm, she worked on marketing and intellectual property. Subsequently, she held public sector positions in the Chicago city government as an Assistant to the Mayor, and as Assistant Commissioner of Planning and Development. In

1993, she became Executive Director for the Chicago office of Public Allies, a non-profit organization encouraging young people to work on social issues in nonprofit groups and government agencies. She worked there nearly four years and set fundraising records for the organization that still stood a dozen years after she left.

In 1996, Obama served as the Associate Dean of Student Services at the University of Chicago, where she developed the University's Community Service Center. In 2002, she began working for the University of Chicago Hospitals, first as executive director for community affairs and, beginning May, 2005, as Vice President for Community and External Affairs. She continued to hold the position during the primary campaign, but cut back to part time in order to spend time with her daughters as well as work for her husband's election; she subsequently took a leave of absence from her job.

She served as a salaried board member of TreeHouse Foods, Inc., a major Wal-Mart supplier with whom she cut ties immediately after her husband made comments critical of Wal-Mart at an AFL-CIO forum in Trenton, New Jersey, on May 14, 2007. She serves on the board of directors of the Chicago Council on Global Affairs.

According to the couple's 2006 income tax return, Michelle's salary was $273,618 from the University of Chicago Hospitals, while he had a salary of $157,082 from the United States Senate. The total Obama income, however, was $991,296 including $51,200 she earned as a member of the board of directors of TreeHouse Foods, plus investments and royalties from his books.

Oprah Winfrey joins the Obamas on the campaign trail, December 10, 2007.

With the ascent of her husband as a prominent national politician, she has become a part of pop culture. In May 2006, Essence magazine listed her among "25 of the World`s Most Inspiring Women." In July 2007, Vanity Fair magazine listed her among "10 of the World`s Best Dressed People." She was a honorary guest at Oprah Winfrey`s Legends Ball as an "young`un" paying tribute to the ´Legends,` which helped pave the way for African American Women. In September 2007, 02138 magazine listed her 58th of "The Harvard 100," a list of the prior year`s most influential Harvard alumni. Her husband was ranked fourth. In July 2008, she made a repeat appearance on the Vanity Fair international best dressed list. She also appeared on the 2008 People list of best-dressed women and was praised by the magazine for her "classic and confident" look. Some sources compare her to Jacqueline Kennedy due to her sleek but not overdone style, and other sources such as the New York Times compare her to Barbara Bush as well not only for her fashion sense, but also for her demeanor because she is known for her discipline and decorum. Her fashion sense generally outpolled those of Cindy McCain and Sarah Palin during the 2008 Presidential Election race.

Obama`s package of attributes is anticipated to be well-suited for the role of First Lady by some. She often wears clothes by designers Calvin Klein,Oscar de la Renta,Isabel Toledo, Narciso Rodriguez, Donna Ricco and Maria Pinto.

There was no active undergraduate chapter of Alpha Kappa Alpha at Princeton when Ms. Obama attended. In July 2008, Obama accepted the invitation to become an honorary member of the 100-year-old black sorority.

2008 Presidential election
Campaigning for Barack Obama

Michelle Obama speaking at a campaign event in Plymouth, NH.

Although Michelle Obama has campaigned on her husband`s behalf since early in his political career by handshaking and fund-raising, she did not relish the activity at first. While campaigning during Barack Obama`s 2000 run for U.S. House of Representatives, her boss at the University of Chicago asked if there was any single thing about campaigning that she enjoyed; after some thought, she replied visiting so many living rooms had given her some new decorating ideas.

In May 2007, three months after her husband declared his presidential candidacy, she reduced her professional responsibilities by eighty percent to support his presidential campaign. Early in the campaign, she had limited involvement in which she traveled to political events only two days a week and traveled overnight only if their daughters could come along. In early February 2008, she attended thirty-three events in eight days. She has made at least two campaign appearances with Oprah Winfrey.

In 2007, Michelle gave stump speeches for her husband's presidential campaign at various locations in the United States. Jennifer Hunter of the Chicago Sun-Times wrote about one speech of hers in Iowa, "Michelle was a firebrand, expressing a determined passion for her husband's campaign, talking straight from the heart with eloquence and intelligence."She employs an all-female staff of aides for her political role. She says that she negotiated an agreement in which her husband gave up smoking in exchange for her support of his decision to run. About her role in her husband's presidential campaign she has said: "My job is not a senior adviser."During the campaign, she has discussed race and education by using motherhood as a framework.

This is her first election year on the national political scene and even before the field of Democratic candidates was narrowed to two she was considered the least famous of the candidates' spouses. Early in the campaign, she exhibited her ironic humor and told anecdotes about the Obama family life. However, as the press began to emphasize her sarcasm, which did not translate well in the print media, she toned it down. A New York Times op-ed columnist, Maureen Dowd, wrote:

I wince a bit when Michelle Obama chides her husband as a

mere mortal — comic routine that rests on the presumption that we see him as a god ... But it may not be smart politics to mock him in a way that turns him from the glam JFK into the mundane Gerald Ford, toasting his own English muffin. If all Senator Obama is peddling is the Camelot mystique, why debunk this mystique?

Asked in February 2008 whether she could see herself "working to support" Hillary Clinton if she got the nomination, Michelle said "I`d have to think about that. I`d have to think about policies, her approach, her tone." When questioned about this by the interviewer, however, she stated "You know, everyone in this party is going to work hard for whoever the nominee is."

**The Obamas, with Joe and Jill Biden
at the Vice Presidential announcement
in Springfield, Illinois.**

Despite her criticisms of Clinton during the 2008 campaign, when asked in 2004 which political spouse she admired, Obama cited Hillary Clinton, stating, "She is smart and gracious and everything she appears to be in public — someone who`s managed to raise what appears to be a solid, grounded child."

On October 6, 2008 Larry King Live Obama was asked if the American electorate is past the Bradley effect. She stated that

Barack's achievement of the nomination was a fairly strong indicator that it is. The same night she also was interviewed by Jon Stewart on the Daily Show where she deflected criticism of her husband and his campaign. Her first Daily Show appearance came after her husband had made three such appearances.

The following weekend, the Obamas held a high-priced fundraiser for the Presidential campaign and for the Democratic National Committee to raise money from women. Obama has also been courting working women.

Her assigned Secret Service codename is "Renaissance"
Criticism for "For the first time in my life" comments

On February 18, 2008, Obama commented in Milwaukee, Wisconsin that "For the first time in my adult life, I am proud of my country because it feels like hope is finally making a comeback." Later that evening she reworded her stump speech in Madison, Wisconsin, saying "For the first time in my adult lifetime, I'm really proud of my country, and not just because Barack has done well, but because I think people are hungry for change." Several commentators criticized her remarks, and the campaign issued a statement that "anyone who heard her remarks ... would understand that she was commenting on our politics." In June 2008 Laura Bush indicated she thought Michelle Obama's words had been misrepresented in the media "I think she probably meant I`m ´more proud,` you know, is what she really meant," adding, "I mean, I know that, and that`s one of the things you learn and that`s one of the really difficult parts both of running for president and for being the spouse of the president, and that is, everything you say is looked at and in many cases misconstrued."

Throughout the campaign, the media have often labeled Obama as an "angry black woman," and some websites have attempted to propagate this perception, causing her to respond:

Barack and I have been in the public eye for many years now, and we`ve developed a thick skin along the way. When you're out campaigning, there will always be criticism. I just take it in stride, and at the end of the day, I know that it comes with the territory."

By the time of the 2008 Democratic National Convention in August, media outlets observed Obama`s presence on the campaign trail had grown softer than at the start of the race, focusing on soliciting concerns and empathizing with audience rather than throwing down challenges to them, and giving interviews to shows like The View and publications like Ladies` Home Journal rather than appearing on news programs. The change was even reflected in her fashion choices, with Obama wearing more and more sundresses in place of her previous designer pieces. The View appearance was partly intended to help soften the perception of her, and it was widely-covered in the press.

Democratic National Convention speech
at the 2008 Democratic National Convention

Michelle Obama was regarded as a charismatic public speaker from the very beginning of the campaign. She delivered the keynote address on the first night of the 2008 Democratic National Convention on August 25, during which she sought to portray herself and her family as the embodiment of the American Dream. Other speakers that night included Jesse Jackson, Jr. and Edward Kennedy, who some expected to steal the limelight. She described Barack as a family man and herself as no different from many women; she also spoke about the backgrounds that she and her husband came from. Obama said both she and her husband believed "that you work hard for what you want in life, that your word is your bond, and you do what you say you`re going to do, that you treat people with dignity and respect, even if you don`t know them, and even if you don`t agree with them." She also emphasized her love of country, in response to criticism for her previous statements about feeling proud of her country for the first time. Her daughters joined her on the stage after the speech and greeted their father, who appeared on the overhead video screen.

Obama`s speech was largely well received and drew mostly positive reviews. A Rasmussen Reports poll found that her favorablity among Americans reached 55%. Political commentator Andrew Sullivan described the speech as "one of the best, most moving, intimate, rousing, humble, and beautiful speeches I've heard from a convention platform." Ezra Klein of The American Prospect, described it as a "beautifully delivered, and smartly crafted, speech" and described Obama as "coming off as wholesome and, frankly, familiar." Katherine Marsh of The New Republic, however, said she missed "the old Michelle... not the Stepford wife fist-bumping Elisabeth Hasselbeck, but the sassy better half who reminded us that while Barack was the answer, he was also stinky in the morning and forgot to put the butter away. She both affirmed his promise and humanized him." Jason Zengerle, also of The New Republic, said Obama should have emphasized her professional and educational achievements as well as her mother, daughter and sister qualities; Zengerle wrote, "It almost makes you long for the days when politicians' wives were seen but not heard. After all, if they're not permitted to really say anything, what's the point of having them speak."Time described the evening's series of speakers as the long awaited passing of the torch from the long line of Kennedy family members to the next man to be the Democratic Party standard bearer.

**Remarks of Michelle Obama
to the Democratic National Committee`s
Gay and Lesbian Leadership Committee**

New York City, NY | June 26, 2008

I would like to acknowledge Governor Dean for all his hard work building our party. He is delayed this evening – had flight trouble – but should be arriving shortly. I know we`re looking forward to hearing from him, and we are proud to have him as our party Chairman.

I also want to recognize the members of UNITE HERE Local 6 who are working this event tonight. And thank you all for inviting me to spend some time with you.

I`m honored to be with you in a week that reminds us just how far we`ve come as a country. Five years ago today, the Supreme Court delivered justice with the decision in Lawrence v. Texas that same-sex couples would never again be persecuted through use of criminal law. And on Saturday, we recognize the anniversary of the day people stood up at Stonewall and said "enough."

These anniversaries remind us that no matter who we are, or where we come from, or what we look like, we are only here because of the brave efforts of those who came before us. That we are all only here because of those who marched and bled and died, from Selma to Stonewall, in a pursuit of that more perfect union that is the promise of this country.

Over the course of this campaign, we've seen a fundamental change in the level of political engagement in this country.

We've seen a renewed sense of possibility and a hunger for change. We've seen people of all ages and backgrounds investing time and energy like never before; writing $20, $30, $50 checks; investing for the first time ever in a political candidate. We've seen people talking to their neighbors about candidates and issues; working hard to clarify misperceptions; challenging one another to think differently about the world and our place in it.

It's precisely this type of individual engagement and investment that has been the mission of my husband's life. Barack has always believed that there is more in this country that unites us than divides us; that our common stories and struggles and values are what make this country great; that meaningful change never happens from the top down but from the bottom up.

I'll never forget the first time I realized there was something special about Barack. It was nearly 20 years ago this summer. Barack and I were just getting to know one another, and he thought the best way for me to get to know him better was to get a better sense of the work he cared about most - his work as a community organizer.

He took me to a small church basement on the South Side of Chicago, where a group of neighborhood residents were gathered; folks he knew from his years as a community organizer before he went to law school. They were desperate for change. They were regular Americans struggling to build a decent life for themselves and their families.

Single mothers living paycheck to paycheck; grandparents raising grandkids despite an income that wouldn't allow it; men unable to support their families because jobs had disappeared when steel mills closed. Like most Americans, they didn't want much; they weren't asking for much: just dignity and respect.

I watched as Barack walked into the room, took off his jacket, rolled up his sleeves, and instantly connected with each and every person in that room. He spoke eloquently of "the world as it is" and "the world as it should be."

He said the key to change is understanding that our job as

citizens of this nation is to work hard each and every day to narrow the gap between those two ideas. He explained that we often settle for the world as it is even if it doesn`t reflect our personal values.

But he reminded us that it is only through determination and hard work that we slowly make the world as it is and the world as it should be one in the same. His words were powerful not only because they made us believe in him - they challenged each of us to believe in ourselves.

One of the many reasons I`m proud of the way Barack has handled himself in this campaign is that he is still the same man I fell in love with in that church basement. His unyielding belief in that simple idea – closing the gap between the world as it is and the world as it should be - is precisely why he`ll be a President you can be proud of.

Barack is not new to the cause of the LGBT community. It has been a conviction of his career since he was first elected to public office. In his first year in the Illinois State Senate, he cosponsored a bill amending the Illinois Human Rights Act to include protections for LGBT men and women.

He worked on that bill for seven years, serving as chief co-sponsor and lobbying his colleagues to reject the political expedience of homophobia and make LGBT equality a priority.

In 2004, his efforts paid off as that bill finally became law, prohibiting discrimination on the basis of both sexual orientation and gender identity in the workplace, in housing, and in public places.

He's led on gender-based violence with his work on the Illinois Gender Violence Act, successfully reaching across the aisle to put in place the nation's strongest law giving the survivors of sexual assault or domestic violence legal remedy against their attackers. He joined his colleagues in fighting to include explicit protections for the LGBT community in that act. He lost that battle, but his efforts brought gender violence in the LGBT community into the political consciousness like never before.

In 2004, after hearing from gay friends and supporters about the hurtful impact of DOMA, Barack went on record during his U.S. Senate race calling for its complete repeal. And as a U.S. Senator, he voted to protect our Constitution from the stain of discrimination by voting against the Federal Marriage Amendment.

Barack's record is clear. There is so much at stake in this election. The direction of our country hangs in the balance. We are faced with those two clear choices: The world as it is, and the world as it should be. We have to ask ourselves: Are we willing to settle for the world as it is or are we willing to work for the world as it should be?

Despite the extraordinary challenges we face today, we have a candidate who believes that the country is moving in the right direction, despite the inequalities created over the last 8 years.

And then we have Barack Obama, who believes that we must fight for the world as it should be.

A world where together we work to reverse discriminatory laws like DOMA and Don`t Ask, Don`t Tell.

A world where LGBT Americans get a fair shake at working hard to get ahead without workplace discrimination.

A world where our federal government fully protects all of us – including LGBT Americans - from hate crimes.

And, a world where our federal laws don`t discriminate against same-sex relationships, including equal treatment for any relationship recognized under state law.

A world that recognizes that equality in relationship, family, and adoption rights is not some abstract principle; it`s about whether millions of LGBT Americans can finally live lives marked by dignity and freedom. Barack has made crystal clear his commitment to ensuring full equality for LGBT couples.

That is why he supports robust civil unions. That is why he has said that the federal government should not stand in the way of states that want to decide for themselves how best to pursue equality for gay and lesbian couples -- whether that means a domestic partnership, a civil union, or a civil marriage.

And that is why he opposes all divisive and discriminatory constitutional amendments – whether it`s a proposed amendment to the California and Florida Constitutions or the U.S. Constitution. Because the world as it should be rejects discrimination.

But, it`s not just about the positions you take, it`s also about the leadership you provide.

Barack`s got the courage to talk to skeptical audiences; not just friendly ones. That`s why he told a crowd at a rally in Texas that gays and lesbians deserve equality. Now, the crowd got pretty quiet.

But Barack said "now, I`m a Christian, and I praise Jesus every Sunday." And the crowd started cheering. Then he said, "I hear people saying things that I don`t think are very Christian with respect to people who are gay and lesbian." And you know what? The crowd kept cheering.

That's why he told evangelicals at Rick Warren's Saddleback church that we need a renewed call to action on HIV and AIDS.

That's why he went to Ebenezer Baptist Church and said that we need to get over homophobia in the African-American community; that if we're honest with ourselves, we'll embrace our gay brothers and sisters instead of scorning them. And that's why he stood up at the 2004 Democratic National Convention and told all of America that we refuse to be divided anymore.

That's the choice in this election. Between slipping backward and moving forward. Between being timid or being courageous. Between fighting for the world as it should be, or settling for the world as it is.

My husband is running for President to build an America that lives up to the ideals written into our Constitution. We have just come through a historic primary election where a woman and a black man were running to become President of the United States. It hasn't been painless, but change never is. As I travel this country, I am certain that we have arrived at a moment in our collective history where we are ready to move forward and create the "world as it should be."

I know which world Barack will fight for each and every day

as your President. But he can`t do it alone. As he said in that church basement, change happens when ordinary people are ready to take the reins of their own destiny. He needs you by his side every step of the way. That kind of change won`t be easy. There will be powerful forces who believe that things should stay just the way they are.

That`s where you come in. Your voices of truth and hope and of possibility have to drown out the skeptics and the cynics.

If you stand with my husband; if you reach for what is possible and if you refuse to let this chance get away; we can begin building that better world in November.

Thank you.

Remarks of Michelle Obama
Democratic National Convention

Denver, CO | August 25, 2008

As you might imagine, for Barack, running for President is nothing compared to that first game of basketball with my brother Craig.

I can`t tell you how much it means to have Craig and my mom here tonight. Like Craig, I can feel my dad looking down on us, just as I`ve felt his presence in every grace-filled moment of my life.

At six-foot-six, I`ve often felt like Craig was looking down on me too... literally. But the truth is, both when we were kids and today, he wasn`t looking down on me - he was watching over me.

And he's been there for me every step of the way since that clear February day 19 months ago, when - with little more than our faith in each other and a hunger for change - we joined my husband, Barack Obama, on the improbable journey that's brought us to this moment.

But each of us also comes here tonight by way of our own improbable journey.

I come here tonight as a sister, blessed with a brother who is my mentor, my protector and my lifelong friend.

I come here as a wife who loves my husband and believes he will be an extraordinary president.

I come here as a Mom whose girls are the heart of my heart and the center of my world - they're the first thing I think about when I wake up in the morning, and the last thing I think about when I go to bed at night. Their future - and all our children's future - is my stake in this election.

And I come here as a daughter - raised on the South Side of Chicago by a father who was a blue collar city worker, and a mother who stayed at home with my brother and me. My mother's love has always been a sustaining force for our family, and one of my greatest joys is seeing her integrity, her compassion, and her intelligence reflected in my own daughters.

My Dad was our rock. Although he was diagnosed with Multiple Sclerosis in his early thirties, he was our provider, our champion, our hero. As he got sicker, it got harder for him to walk, it took him longer to get dressed in the morning. But if he was in pain, he never let on. He never stopped smiling and laughing - even while struggling to button his shirt, even while using two canes to get himself across the room to give my Mom a kiss. He just woke up a little earlier, and worked a little harder.

He and my mom poured everything they had into me and Craig. It was the greatest gift a child can receive: never doubting for a single minute that you`re loved, and cherished, and have a place in this world. And thanks to their faith and hard work, we both were able to go on to college. So I know firsthand from their lives - and mine - that the American Dream endures.

And you know, what struck me when I first met Barack was that even though he had this funny name, even though he`d grown up all the way across the continent in Hawaii, his family was so much like mine. He was raised by grandparents who were working class folks just like my parents, and by a single mother who struggled to pay the bills just like we did. Like my family, they scrimped and saved so that he could have opportunities they never had themselves. And Barack and I were raised with so many of the same values: that you work hard for what you want in life; that your word is your bond and you do what you say you`re going to do; that you treat people with dignity and respect, even if you don`t know them, and even if you don`t agree with them.

And Barack and I set out to build lives guided by these values, and pass them on to the next generation. Because we want our children - and all children in this nation - to know that the only limit to the height of your achievements is the reach of your dreams and your willingness to work for them.

And as our friendship grew, and I learned more about Barack, he introduced me to the work he`d done when he first moved to Chicago after college. Instead of heading to Wall Street, Barack had gone to work in neighborhoods devastated when steel plants shut down, and jobs dried up. And he`d been invited back to speak to people from those neighborhoods about how to rebuild their community.

The people gathered together that day were ordinary folks doing the best they could to build a good life. They were parents living paycheck to paycheck; grandparents trying to get by on a fixed income; men frustrated that they couldn`t support their families after their jobs disappeared. Those folks weren`t asking for a handout or a shortcut. They were ready to work - they wanted to contribute. They believed - like you and I believe - that America should be a place where you can make it if you try.

Barack stood up that day, and spoke words that have stayed with me ever since. He talked about "The world as it is" and "The world as it should be." And he said that all too often, we accept the distance between the two, and settle for the world as it is - even when it doesn't reflect our values and aspirations. But he reminded us that we know what our world should look like. We know what fairness and justice and opportunity look like. And he urged us to believe in ourselves - to find the strength within ourselves to strive for the world as it should be. And isn't that the great American story?

It's the story of men and women gathered in churches and union halls, in town squares and high school gyms - people who stood up and marched and risked everything they had - refusing to settle, determined to mold our future into the shape of our ideals.

It is because of their will and determination that this week, we celebrate two anniversaries: the 88th anniversary of women winning the right to vote, and the 45th anniversary of that hot summer day when Dr. King lifted our sights and our hearts with his dream for our nation.

I stand here today at the crosscurrents of that history - knowing that my piece of the American Dream is a blessing hard won by those who came before me. All of them driven by the same conviction that drove my dad to get up an hour early each day to painstakingly dress himself for work. The same conviction that drives the men and women I`ve met all across this country:

People who work the day shift, kiss their kids goodnight, and head out for the night shift - without disappointment, without regret - that goodnight kiss a reminder of everything they`re working for.

The military families who say grace each night with an empty seat at the table. The servicemen and women who love this country so much, they leave those they love most to defend it.

The young people across America serving our communities - teaching children, cleaning up neighborhoods, caring for the least among us each and every day.

People like Hillary Clinton, who put those 18 million cracks in the glass ceiling, so that our daughters - and sons - can dream a little bigger and aim a little higher.

People like Joe Biden, who`s never forgotten where he came from, and never stopped fighting for folks who work long hours and face long odds and need someone on their side again.

All of us driven by a simple belief that the world as it is just won`t do - that we have an obligation to fight for the world as it should be.

That is the thread that connects our hearts. That is the thread that runs through my journey and Barack`s journey and so many other improbable journeys that have brought us here tonight, where the current of history meets this new tide of hope.

That is why I love this country.

And in my own life, in my own small way, I`ve tried to give back to this country that has given me so much. That`s why I left a job at a law firm for a career in public service, working to empower young people to volunteer in their communities. Because I believe that each of us - no matter what our age or background or walk of life - each of us has something to contribute to the life of this nation.

It`s a belief Barack shares - a belief at the heart of his life`s work.

It`s what he did all those years ago, on the streets of Chicago, setting up job training to get people back to work and after school programs to keep kids safe - working block by block to help people lift up their families.

It`s what he did in the Illinois Senate, moving people from welfare to jobs, passing tax cuts for hard working families, and making sure women get equal pay for equal work.

It`s what he`s done in the United States Senate, fighting to ensure the men and women who serve this country are welcomed home not just with medals and parades, but with good jobs and benefits and health care - including mental health care.

That`s why he`s running - to end the war in Iraq responsibly, to build an economy that lifts every family, to make health care available for every American, and to make sure every child in this nation gets a world class education all the way from preschool to college. That`s what Barack Obama will do as President of the United States of America.

He`ll achieve these goals the same way he always has - by bringing us together and reminding us how much we share and how alike we really are. You see, Barack doesn`t care where you`re from, or what your background is, or what party - if any - you belong to. That`s not how he sees the world. He knows that thread that connects us - our belief in America`s promise, our commitment to our children`s future - is strong enough to hold us together as one nation even when we disagree.

It was strong enough to bring hope to those neighborhoods in Chicago.

It was strong enough to bring hope to the mother he met worried about her child in Iraq; hope to the man who`s unemployed, but can`t afford gas to find a job; hope to the student working nights to pay for her sister`s health care, sleeping just a few hours a day.

And it was strong enough to bring hope to people who came out on a cold Iowa night and became the first voices in this chorus for change that`s been echoed by millions of Americans from every corner of this nation.

Millions of Americans who know that Barack understands their dreams; that Barack will fight for people like them; and that Barack will finally bring the change we need.

And in the end, after all that`s happened these past 19 months, the Barack Obama I know today is the same man I fell in love with 19 years ago. He`s the same man who drove me and our new baby daughter home from the hospital ten years ago this summer, inching along at a snail`s pace, peering anxiously at us in the rearview mirror, feeling the whole weight of her future in his hands, determined to give her everything he'd struggled so hard for himself, determined to give her what he never had: the affirming embrace of a father's love.

And as I tuck that little girl and her little sister into bed at night, I think about how one day, they'll have families of their own. And one day, they - and your sons and daughters - will tell their own children about what we did together in this election. They'll tell them how this time, we listened to our hopes, instead of our fears. How this time, we decided to stop doubting and to start dreaming. How this time, in this great country - where a girl from the South Side of Chicago can go to college and law school, and the son of a single mother from Hawaii can go all the way to the White House - we committed ourselves to building the world as it should be.

So tonight, in honor of my father's memory and my daughters' future - out of gratitude to those whose triumphs we mark this week, and those whose everyday sacrifices have brought us to this moment - let us devote ourselves to finishing their work; let us work together to fulfill their hopes; and let us stand together to elect Barack Obama President of the United States of America.

Thank you, God bless you, and God bless America.

Remarks of Michelle Obama
North Carolina Economic Roundtable
with Working Women

Charlotte, NC | September 18, 2008

I want to thank Elaine Marshall for joining us today. Over 10 years ago, you broke barriers here in North Carolina, by becoming the first woman elected to a statewide executive office. And during your time as secretary of state, you've been such a strong advocate for women and children. Thank you for bringing your experiences to our conversation today.

I'm also joined by four women from right here in Charlotte. Today, we're talking about issues that they know very well, because they live these issues every day. They are Essie Reynolds, Stacy Branning, Betsy Olinger, and Deanna Boskovich. Thank you for joining us to share your stories.

It's great to be here, to have this chance to talk about the issues that are always on my mind, and that I know are on your minds... the issues that matter most to women and families.

43

Like many of you, and like women I've met all across the country, I juggle several different roles in my life. I'm a wife, I'm a working woman, I'm a daughter, a sister and a friend.

But most importantly, I'm a mom. My girls are the first thing I think about when I wake up in the morning and the last thing I think about when I go to bed at night. No matter where I am- at work, on the campaign trail, you name it-they're always on my mind.

So for me, policies that support working women and families aren't just political issues. They're personal. They're the causes I carry in my heart every single day.

I'm always amazed at how different things are for working families today than when I was growing up. When I was a kid, my father, a blue-collar city worker, could earn enough from his job to support our whole family, while my mother stayed home to take care of my brother and me. But today, one income-especially a shift worker's income like my dad's-just doesn't cut it. In most families, both parents have to work.

And it's even harder for single parents. Here in North Carolina, roughly one in eight households are run by single women-folks who often have to work more than one job to make ends meet. And that's not counting the jobs you do when the workday is done and the kids are in bed - jobs like doing the laundry, and packing those lunches, and fixing the house. And when the bills keep piling up, and that list of chores seems endless, many of us find ourselves doing yet another job - worrying late into the night.

Now, I know that if you ask anyone here, they'd agree that caring for their families is the greatest joy of their lives. They wouldn't trade it for anything. We all know that being a parent is the best job in the world - most days, at least.

But as Barack and I have traveled this country over the past year and a half, we've heard from so many parents who are working as hard as they can to do it all, but just can't seem to get ahead.

Each of the women up on this stage has a unique story. But all of their stories point to a common trend. Working women and families are shouldering an enormous burden, and they carry it with pride and without complaint. But that load shouldn't be so heavy - and they shouldn't have to bear it all by themselves.

That's what this election is about for Barack and for me...the families who are doing everything asked of them and more.

And they're not asking for the government to solve all their problems. They're just asking for Washington to understand what`s happening to their families and to be on their side for a change.

This is something that Barack understands very well, because he`s been there.

Barack was raised by a young single mom who put herself through school. She was determined to show him that there are no barriers to your success if you`re willing to work for it. But he also saw her struggle to make ends meet, at times worrying about how she would pay the bills.

Barack and I both were lucky enough to go to college and law school. But our education came at a cost. We just finished paying off our student loans a few years ago. So we know how it feels to carry debt.

And Barack has seen firsthand how people are impacted when the economy suffers. He spent years working in neighborhoods in Chicago that were devastated when steel plants shut down and jobs dried up. That`s why he`s worked hard to create new jobs and reform our schools, to give our young people the skills they need to succeed in this economy.

Barack gets it. He understands that people aren`t asking for much. They just want policies that help them in their everyday lives. Policies that give them a chance to work hard and get ahead. They're looking for a Washington that doesn't stand in their way.

So on Election Day, we have a choice to make. And when I look at the two candidates and their plans for America's future, and when I think about all the families I've met across the country, and the kind of help they could use right now, the choice is clear.

Barack is the only candidate in this election who has built his economic plan around the middle class, by giving a tax cut to 95 percent of all working Americans, rewarding companies that create jobs here in America, and ensuring that women are paid fairly for our work. In North Carolina, women make just 82 cents for every dollar that a man earns. Over the course of a lifetime, that adds up to tens of thousands of dollars - money people could be spending on gas and groceries and saving for college. Barack is determined to close that pay gap once and for all.

He's the only candidate with a health plan that will cover all Americans and save families up to $2,500, and require insurance companies to cover preventive care and stop turning their backs on people with pre-existing conditions.

Barack is the only candidate who has a long-term energy plan that looks beyond quick fixes and makes real investments in renewable energy, to end our dependence on foreign oil and protect our planet for our kids and grandkids.

He's the only candidate with a comprehensive plan to invest in our schools, by strengthening early childhood education, recruiting an army of new teachers, and making college affordable for students from all different backgrounds.

He's the only candidate who will expand the Family and Medical Leave Act and require employers to provide workers with at least seven paid sick days a year. Because he believes, like you and I believe, that it's unacceptable that twenty-two million working women don't have a single paid sick day. People shouldn't be fired for getting sick or staying home to care for a sick child or parent. That's not who we are.

And Barack is the only candidate who has a timeline for bringing our troops home from Iraq responsibly, so that we can rebuild our military and start investing the $10 billion we're spending each month in Iraq right here at home.

This is the choice we face. These policies - Barack's policies - are the change we need. In the end, Barack is determined to change Washington, so that instead of just talking about family values, we actually have policies that value families.

That's why I'm here today. I'm here for my daughters' future-

and all our children`s future. They`re my stake in this election. I`m here today because I want to leave them a better world-a world where they`ll have opportunities that we and our mothers and grandmothers could only dream of.

That`s the choice we face in this election: whether we`ll start building that better world right now, or have another four years that look just like the last eight.

And making that choice begins with understanding what`s really happening with America`s families.

So I`d like to turn the conversation to our guests here, to learn more about what`s going on with their lives, their kids, their jobs, what`s working, what`s not working, and where they could use some extra help in getting it all done.

Remarks of Michelle Obama
Roundtable Discussion
with Pennsylvania Military Spouses

Allentown, PA | September 24, 2008

I`m delighted to be here today with Jill. She`s my partner on this campaign, she`s a proud military mom, and she`s a strong supporter of military families across Delaware. I know I can speak for both of us when I say, it`s a pleasure to be here today with all of you.

And thank you, General Lenhardt, for the years of service you have given to our country - most recently, as the legendary Sergeant-at-Arms for the U.S. Senate. Thank you for being here today.

We`re also joined by three women from right here in the Allentown region. Today, we`ll talk about issues that they know very well because they live these issues every day. They are Carol Reese, Kathleen Miller, and Jill Slivka. Thank you all for joining us today and sharing your stories.

It`s an honor to visit a state that has sent so many of its sons and daughters, husbands and wives, and mothers and fathers to protect our nation in the military.

Today, 4,000 troops from the Pennsylvania Army National Guard`s Stryker Brigade are mobilizing for duty in Iraq. They are among the 19,000 National Guard personnel who live throughout the state... many of whom have been deployed since September 11th. And more than 1 million veterans call Pennsylvania home.

I know that, today, we`re all thinking about the troops, as we talk about the families that they are thinking about every day.

These roundtables are one of my favorite things to do on the campaign trail. I treasure these opportunities to hear your stories, about your lives, your families, and the unique challenges you face every day.

One thing that is very clear from these conversations is the pride that families like yours feel. Pride in your country, pride in your family, and pride in the service that you and your loved ones are giving to the United States.

Your pride is well-deserved. I`m honored to be here with all of you. And Barack and I, and all Americans, are so grateful for the sacrifices you make every day to serve our country.

The women up here with me each have their own perspective on the issues that matter most to their lives, whether it`s a more efficient VA system or TRICARE; a better education for their children; or more predictable deployments, so units have time to retrain and re-equip, and families have time to reconnect.

But all of these folks have some fundamental things in common. They all know what it`s like to balance work with raising their kids while their spouses are away. And they are united in a vision we all share: of a system that does more to support its military families, both when a spouse is deployed, and long after he or she returns.

And everyone on this stage and everyone in this room share something else as well. We`ve all been touched by the economic crisis that our nation is facing. And I know that all of you are feeling the effects every day.

You`re feeling it when you pay for gas and groceries. You feel it when you worry about how you'll afford college for your kids and retirement for yourselves, because we all know that incomes aren't keeping up with rising costs. You're lucky if your income is standing still.

And you feel it when you wonder if you'll still have your job this time next year. So many people throughout the Lehigh Valley have lost their jobs. People who spent years working in manufacturing and retail and transportation. And you feel it when you worry about whether you'll be able to pay the mortgage this month. Because in just the past few months, more than 10,000 families across Pennsylvania went to their mailboxes and found foreclosure notices on their homes.

Most of all, you feel it when you tuck your kids in at night and wonder what kind of world we're going to be leaving for them. That's a thought I know all of us carry in our hearts every day.

And all of these challenges are even harder for military spouses. You become everything while your spouse is away. You're Mom and Dad. You're in charge of the checkbook. You're looking after your in-laws. You're making dinner and helping with homework. You're doling out discipline. And when the bills keep piling up, and that list of chores seems endless, you find yourself with yet another job: worrying late into the night.

As Barack and I have traveled to every corner of this country during the past 19 months, we've heard from so many military spouses who are working hard to do it all without the support they deserve.

And if there's one thing I've learned from these roundtables, it's that when our military goes to war, their families go with them.

And I know that your marriages face unique challenges. Your spouses may be deployed for months at a time, in the toughest conditions imaginable. They may come home with problems you're simply not equipped to deal with, and there can be a stigma attached to asking for help. Or they come home, life is good, but there's a readjustment period, and as soon as you get back to where you were before, the bags are packed for another deployment.

But what has also struck me in my conversations with military spouses is how you all take care of each other. Barack and I can see how the military really is like a family. You fill in where services fail, from baby-sitting to untangling bureaucracies to delivering bad news. Even if you aren't trained for it or prepared for it, you do it. You have to.

I'll never forget a moment from one of these roundtables, when a young mother started pouring out how overwhelmed she felt. We all sat there together and listened to her. And when she finished, another woman stood up and said, "I don't know you. But when you leave here, you will have my phone number. And you will be able to call me anytime. You've got the support of this friend right here."

That's the kind of strength that we see from military spouses across the country every day. They're doing everything that's asked of them and more. And they're not asking for much in return. They're not asking for Washington to solve all their problems. They're just asking for Washington to understand the challenges that their families face, as part of their extraordinary commitment to our country.

Well, Barack understands it. His life was shaped by the sacred contract our country makes with the men and women who serve.

Barack's grandfather enlisted after Pearl Harbor. He marched in Patton's Army. Barack's grandmother worked on a bomber assembly line while her husband was away. And Barack's mother was born at Fort Leavenworth.

When his grandfather returned to America, our country rewarded his service with the opportunity to go to college on the GI Bill. He was able to buy his first home with a loan from the Federal Housing Administration, and move his family west, all the way to Hawaii, where he and Barack's grandmother helped raise him.

And today, Barack is determined to lead America to make that same commitment to military families so other families can have the opportunities that his family did.

That's why, when he arrived in the Senate, Barack sought a seat on the Veterans Affairs Committee. He led a bipartisan effort to improve care at Walter Reed, because recovering servicemen should go to the front of the line, and they shouldn't have to fight to get there. He helped pass laws that gave family members health care and a year of job protection, so they never have to choose between caring for a loved one and keeping a job.

Now these issues are at stake in this election. So on November 4th, we have a choice to make.

And when I look at the two candidates and their plans for America, when I think about all the military families I've met across the country, and the kind of help they could use right now and when I think about the future we all want to create for our children the choice is clear.

Barack is the only candidate in this race who wants to create a 21st century VA that offers world-class care and rejects the idea that we should only treat combat injuries, but not those sustained in training or on the deck of an aircraft carrier. And Barack is the only candidate who has a record of strong support for efforts to improve mental health care for service members and veterans.

He's the only candidate who has been a consistent supporter of Senator Webb's 21st Century GI Bill so that service members can share their benefits with their families, and more people can achieve the American Dream. Because all of our troops should get the same opportunity that Barack's grandfather had: an affordable college education.

And Barack is the only candidate in this election who has put the middle class at the heart of his economic plan. He wants to give a tax cut to 95 percent of all working Americans, reward companies that create jobs here in America, and ensure that women are paid fairly for our work.

Barack is the only candidate who will expand the Family and Medical Leave Act to cover reserve families, so that when a reservist is called up, their spouse can take time off work to get their family's affairs in order.

And he's is the only candidate with a plan to responsibly end the war in Iraq and bring our troops home, so we can rebuild our military and start investing the $10 billion we're spending each month in Iraq right here at home.

In the end, Barack is the only candidate determined to change Washington, so that instead of just talking about family values, we actually have policies that value families.

That's the idea at the core of my husband's campaign. That we're all in this together.

Today, I've brought along copies of a blueprint describing the Obama-Biden to support military families. It's also a resource guide of the services available to you here in Pennsylvania to help you find a job, or get the health care or family support you need.

If Barack has the honor of serving as our President, and I have the privilege of serving as your First Lady, I'm going to keep having these conversations with you... and bringing your stories home to him. Because the Commander-in-Chief doesn't only need to know how to lead the military. He also needs to understand what war does to military families, and what he can do to help your families stay healthy and strong.

That's why I'm here today. Thank you for joining me.

Compiled by Susan A. Jones

Cover photo:
Vargas2040

Published 2009 by SoHo Books

Printed in America